Coffee Can Science

25 Easy, Hands-on Activities That Teach Key Concepts in Physical, Earth, and Life Sciences—and Meet the Science Standards

by Steve "The Dirtmeister®" Tomecek

New York • Toronto • London • Auckland • Sydney
New Delhi • Mexico City • Hong Kong • Buenos Aires

Teaching
Resources

Dedication

In memory of my Uncle Joe, who not only taught me to think "outside the box," but always made a great cup of coffee!

Cover and interior design by NEO Grafika
Illustrations by Mike Moran

ISBN 0-439-48259-3
Copyright © 2004 by Steve Tomecek
All rights reserved.
Printed in the U.S.A.

6 7 8 9 10   40   11 10 09 08 07

Table of Contents

Earth and Space Science

Life Science

Introduction

Everywhere you turn these days, it seems that people are coming up with "new and improved" ways of teaching science. While there is an ever-increasing number of high-tech science kits entering the market, they are frequently out of reach of many elementary and middle-school teachers. In these days of budget cuts and expanding rosters many teachers simply don't have the financial resources to purchase these science kits. In addition, manufactured science kits are often designed to work only with a specific, pre-set curriculum, limiting their flexibility. Teachers need activities that use inexpensive materials and can be easily adapted to a variety of classroom situations.

This is exactly what *Coffee Can Science* offers. The 26 science activities in this book are all centered on the use of an empty coffee can, along with its plastic lid, plus a few other easy-to-find materials. With these simple supplies, you and your students can conduct fun and easy hands-on science experiments and projects that cover topics such as sound, energy transfer, erosion, weather, and the human body. While a few of the activities in this book were adapted from previously published ideas, most of the activities are original designs. They have all been developed and tested in actual classroom situations with elementary and middle-school students. Hopefully, you'll find that they will liven up your lessons and give your students the spark that they need to continue learning!

How to Use This Book

Each of the 26 activities in this book comes with its own teaching guide and reproducible activity page. The teaching guide features background information about the key science concepts behind the activity, plus a mini-lesson and demonstration to introduce students to the activity. The reproducible page offers easy step-by-step instructions on how to conduct the experiment, plus critical-thinking questions that invite students to make and write their predictions, record their results, and explain the outcomes of their experiment. A great way to combine science and writing!

There are different ways you can use or present the activities in this book:

✦ You can use the activities as teacher demonstrations to spark students' interest and get them revved up for an upcoming science lesson.

✦ You can have students do the hands-on activities themselves. We suggest dividing the class into small groups and having students work together to conduct the activities.

✦ Another option is to set up "stations" around the classroom and present related activities at the same time. For example, Sonic Blaster, The Resonator, Coffee Can Telephone, Coffee Can Chimes,

Phasers and Croakers, and Coffee Can Guitar are all related to sound. You could set up six stations around the classroom and have groups of students rotate around the stations to try out each activity.

Whichever option you choose, be sure to provide each student with his or her own copy of the activity sheet. This way, each student understands what the activity is about and can record his or her own predictions and observations.

Collecting Cans

It goes without saying that you will need lots of coffee cans. Ask students to bring in empty coffee cans from home, both small (10 to 16 oz) and large (32 to 39 oz), along with their plastic lids. Remove any paper labels on the cans and make sure all the cans are thoroughly washed.

Most of the activities in this book require small coffee cans with their lids, but a few call for large ones. For some of the activities, you'll need to modify the cans as follows:

Small coffee can with the top and bottom removed:
   ✦ Sonic Blaster
   ✦ Potential Energy Can
   ✦ Magnetic Measurement Can
   ✦ Electric Coffee Can
   ✦ Energy Transfer Can

Small coffee can with a hole drilled at the center of the bottom of the can:
   ✦ Coffee Can Telephone
   ✦ Coffee Can Chimes
   ✦ Phasers and Croakers

Small coffee can with two holes drilled at the bottom of the can:
   ✦ Coffee Can Guitar

Large coffee can with a hole drilled at the center of the bottom of the can:
   ✦ Coffee Can Chimes
   ✦ Phasers and Croakers

Large coffee can with the top and bottom removed:
   ✦ Coffee Can Lung

Now that you have your materials ready, it's time to give your students a jolt of *Coffee Can Science*. Enjoy!

National Science Education Standards

The activities in this book meet the following science standards:

Physical Science

For Grades K–4
Properties of Objects and Materials
+ Objects have many observable properties, including temperature. Those properties can be measured using tools, such as thermometers.
+ Objects can be described by the properties of the materials from which they are made.
+ Materials can exist in different states—solid, liquid, and gas. Some materials can be changed from one state to another by heating or cooling.

Position and Motion of Objects
+ The position of an object can be described by locating it relative to another object or the background.
+ The position and motion of objects can be changed by pushing and pulling. The size of the change is related to the strength of the push or pull.
+ Sound is produced by vibrating objects. The pitch of a sound can be varied by changing the rate of vibration.

Light, Heat, Electricity, and Magnetism
+ Heat can be produced in many ways, such as rubbing. Heat can move from one object to another by conduction.
+ Magnets attract and repel each other and certain kinds of other materials.

For Grades 5–8
Properties and Changes of Properties in Matter
+ A substance has characteristic properties, such as a freezing point and a melting point.

Motions and Forces
+ An object that is not being subjected to a force will either stay at rest or continue to move at a constant speed and in a straight line.
+ Unbalanced forces will cause changes in the speed or direction of an object's motion.

Transfer of Energy
+ Energy is a property of many substances and is associated with heat, mechanical motion, and sound. Energy is transferred in many ways.
+ Heat moves in predictable ways, flowing from warmer objects to cooler ones.

✦ A tiny fraction of the light from the sun reaches the earth, transferring energy from the sun to the earth.

For Grades 9–12
Motions and Forces
✦ Objects change their motion only when a net force is applied.

Conservation of Energy and the Increase in Disorder
✦ All energy can be considered to be either kinetic energy, which is the energy of motion, or potential energy, which depends on relative position.

Interactions of Energy and Matter
✦ In some materials, such as metals, electrons flow easily.

Earth and Space Science

For Grades K–4
Properties of Earth Materials
✦ Earth materials are solid rock, soil, and water. The varied materials have different physical properties.

Objects in the Sky
✦ The sun provides the light and heat necessary to maintain the temperature of the earth.

Changes in the Earth and Sky
✦ The surface of the earth changes. Some changes are due to slow processes, such as weathering.
✦ Weather changes from day to day. Weather can be described by measurable quantities, such as temperature and barometric pressure.

For Grades 5–8
Structure of the Earth System
✦ Landforms are the result of constructive and destructive forces. Destructive forces include weathering and erosion.
✦ Soil consists of weathered rocks and decomposed organic material.

Earth in the Solar System
✦ Gravity is the force that governs motion in the solar system. Gravity alone holds us to the earth's surface.
✦ The sun is the major source of energy for changes on the earth's surface.

Life Science

For Grades K–4
The Characteristics of Organisms
- ✦ Each animal has different structures that serve different functions in growth, survival, and reproduction. For example, humans have distinct body structures for breathing.
- ✦ Humans and other organisms have senses that help them detect external cues about their environment.

Organisms and Their Environment
- ✦ All animals depend on plants. Some animals eat plants for food.

For Grades 5–8
Structure and Function in Living Systems
- ✦ Specialized cells perform specialized functions in multicellular organisms.
- ✦ Each type of organ has a distinct structure and set of functions that serve the organism as a whole.
- ✦ The human organism has systems for digestion, respiration, and circulation.

Regulation and Behavior
- ✦ Behavior is one kind of response that an organism can make to an environmental stimulus. Behavioral response is determined in part by heredity and in part from experience.

Diversity and Adaptations of Organisms
- ✦ Species acquire many of their unique characteristics through biological adaptation. Biological adaptations include changes in structures, behaviors, or physiology that enhance survival in a particular environment.

Science and Technology

For Grades K–4
Understanding About Science and Technology
- ✦ People have invented tools and techniques to solve problems.
- ✦ Tools help scientists make better observations and measurements.

Sonic Blaster

Get It Together
- Small empty coffee can with 2 plastic lids (for each group of students)
- Scissors
- Can opener
- Candle with matches or lighter
- Drumstick (or similar-sized wooden stick)

Science Buzz

When you strike an object, you use *mechanical energy* to make it vibrate. The vibrating object causes the air around it to move in a series of sound waves. The harder you hit an object (in other words, the more energy you use), the bigger the vibration and the louder the sound. If you hit an object hard enough, the force of the moving air caused by the vibration is strong enough to blow out a candle flame.

The energy from sound waves makes things move all the time. Sonic booms from airplanes and thunder have been known to shake houses, break windows, and set off car alarms.

Before You Start

Use a can opener to remove the top and bottom from the coffee cans so that you have hollow cylinders. Using scissors, cut a 1-inch-diameter hole in the center of one of the plastic lids. Make a model Sonic Blaster to show your students (see page 11).

What to Do

❶ Set up a candle in front of the room so that the entire class can see it. Make sure that the candle has a stable base and won't tip over.

❷ Invite a student volunteer to assist you. Light the candle and have the volunteer blow on the candle until the flame goes out. Ask: What made the candle go out? *(The breeze from the volunteer's mouth blew it out.)*

❸ Explain to students that when something moves, it uses energy. Energy comes in many different forms. One of the most common forms of energy is called *mechanical energy*. You use it every time you push, pull, or bang on something.

❹ Hold up your Sonic Blaster and the drumstick. Explain that sound is a form of mechanical energy. Walk around the room tapping on the lid of the can. As you do so, ask students to hold their hands in front of the open hole on the lid. Ask: What do you feel? *(They should feel a small puff of air coming out of the can.)*

❺ Photocopy and distribute "Create a Sonic Blaster" (p. 11) to each student. Invite them to make their own Sonic Blaster and record their observations.

Create a Sonic Blaster

Is sound strong enough to bend a piece of cardboard?

❶ Snap the plastic lids on the ends of the coffee can. Make sure that both lids are on tight. Tap on the solid lid a few times with the stick to test it out. You now have a Sonic Blaster!

❷ Fold the card strip about an inch from one end. Tape the strip to the desk so that the long end is standing straight, as shown.

❸ Hold the Sonic Blaster so that the small hole in the bottom lid is about two inches from the card strip. Predict: What do you think will happen when you tap gently on the other end of the can?

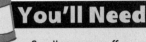

You'll Need

- Small empty coffee can with both ends removed
- 2 plastic coffee-can lids, one with a 1-inch-diameter hole cut out of the center
- Drumstick (or similar-sized wooden stick)
- $1/2$- by 4-inch strip of index card
- Tape

_____

_____

❹ Gently tap on the solid lid. What happened to the card strip?

_____

_____

❺ Predict: What do you think will happen when you bang hard on the solid lid?

_____

_____

❻ Still holding the Sonic Blaster near the card strip, use the stick to bang hard on the solid lid. What happened to the card strip this time?

_____

_____

Think About It: What do you think is the relationship between the loudness of a sound and the amount of energy the sound has?

The Resonator

Get It Together
- Small empty coffee can (for each group of students)
- Several 12-inch round balloons
- Scissors

Science Buzz

When something vibrates it produces a sound. *Frequency* is a measure of how fast an object is vibrating (how many vibrations per second), and it controls the pitch of the sound. The greater the frequency, the higher the pitch.

Sound waves can travel through any type of matter, including air. When a sound wave from one vibrating object hits another object, it can cause it to vibrate as well. Every object has its own natural frequency at which it vibrates best. This is called the *resonant frequency*. If the sound wave created by one vibrating object happens to be the same as the resonant frequency of the second object, then this second object will begin to resonate and vibrate along with it. If you've ever felt the floor shake when a truck rumbles by outside, it's because the truck happens to be hitting one of the resonant frequencies of the building you are in. If a building (or bridge) resonates too much, it can actually collapse!

Before You Start

Use the scissors to cut off the open end of the balloons so you're left with large pieces of curved rubber. Make a model Resonator to show your students (see page 13).

What to Do

❶ Ask students if they've ever seen a demonstration where an opera singer hits a high note, and suddenly a glass nearby starts to shake and finally shatters. Ask: What do you think caused the glass to break? *(The sound of the singer's voice hit the glass and made it shatter.)*

❷ Explain that each sound has its own unique pattern of vibrations. Sometimes a vibration caused by one sound is a perfect match for another object. When this happens, a sound made by one thing can cause something else to vibrate, even if the two aren't touching each other. This is called *resonance*.

❸ Show students your Resonator and explain that they are going to recreate the opera-singer experiment—except instead of breaking a glass, they're going to use the coffee can to make breakfast cereal dance!

❹ Photocopy and distribute "Resonating Away" (p. 13) to each student.

Name _____ **Date** _____

Resonating Away

Use a coffee can and your voice to make breakfast cereal dance!

You'll Need

- Small empty coffee can
- 12-inch round balloon with the open end cut off
- 2 thick rubber bands
- Puffed rice cereal

❶ To make a Resonator, stretch the balloon over the open end of the coffee can. Wrap the rubber bands tightly around the edge of the rubber sheet to secure the balloon. The balloon should be tight like a drum.

❷ Sprinkle about a dozen pieces of puffed cereal on the stretched balloon. Place the can on a table and bring your mouth about six inches from the bottom of the can.

❸ Predict: What do you think will happen to the cereal on the balloon as you begin to sing next to the coffee can?

_____

_____

❹ Begin singing different notes, starting with low notes and moving up to high notes. What happens? Did the same thing happen for every note you sang? What do you think is going on?

_____

_____

_____

_____

Think About It: How do you think resonance works with different objects?

Coffee Can Telephone

Get It Together
- 2 small empty coffee cans (for each pair of students)
- Electric drill or hammer and nail

Science Buzz

Sound travels through all types of matter by causing the material to vibrate in a series of waves. Sound usually travels best through solids because they are often denser than gases or liquids. Not all solids vibrate in the same way, however. Soft solids, like foam rubber, are poor conductors of sound because there is a lot of space between the molecules that make them up. In a similar fashion, a piece of string that is stretched tightly will vibrate more efficiently than one that is held loosely. Sound waves do not lose as much energy when they move along tightly stretched string.

Understanding how different materials vibrate is very important when it comes to controlling sounds. When engineers want to soundproof a room, they line it with material that has a low density and many isolated air spaces. These types of solids make it difficult for vibrations to pass through them.

Before You Start

Use the drill (or hammer and nail) to make a small hole in the center of the bottom of each can. Make a model Coffee Can Telephone to share with students (see page 15).

What to Do

❶ Ask students to hold up a finger about two inches away from their right ear. Using a finger on their other hand, have them scratch the outstretched finger and listen carefully to the sound it makes. Ask them to describe the sound and tell whether it was loud or soft.

❷ Have students repeat the experiment, but this time have them actually touch the outstretched finger to their right ear. After they scratch the finger again, ask: How does the sound compare to the first time you scratched your finger? *(The sound seems louder and deeper.)*

❸ Challenge students to explain what was different about the two trials. *(In the first trial, the sound of the scratching traveled through the air, a gas, while in the second trial, the sound traveled through the bone in the finger, a solid.)*

❹ Explain that sounds travel by means of vibrations, and vibrations usually travel better through solids than through gases, like air. Tell students that they are going to use the vibrations in a solid to make a simple telephone call.

❺ Invite students to create their own Coffee Can Telephone. Photocopy and distribute "Create a Simple Telephone" (p. 15) to each pair of students.

Create a Simple Telephone

How does sound travel through solids?
Build a Coffee Can Telephone and find out!

You'll Need

- 2 small empty coffee cans with a hole drilled into the bottom of each can
- 10- to 15-foot-long string
- 2 large metal washers
- A partner

❶ Thread one end of the string through the bottom of one coffee can and tie the string around a metal washer inside the can. The washer will keep the string from slipping out of the can. Repeat with the other end of the string and the second can. Give one can to your partner and stretch out the string so that it is tight.

❷ Pluck the string a few times. What happens to the string? What do you think is going on?

_____

_____

❸ Repeat Step 2, only this time take a step toward your partner so that the string hangs loosely between the two cans. What do you think will happen to the string when you pluck it this time?

_____

_____

❹ Stretch the string between the cans so that it is tight again. Have your partner place the can to his or her ear while you begin speaking into your can. Can your partner hear what you're saying? Reverse roles so that you do the listening and your partner does the speaking. How is sound traveling between the two cans? Write your ideas here:

_____

_____

❺ Predict: What do you think will happen to your telephone messages if you let the string between the cans go slack again? Write your prediction here, then try it out to see if your prediction was correct!

_____

_____

Think About It: Why do you think sound usually travels better through stiff solids than soft solids?

Coffee Can Chimes

Get It Together
- Small empty coffee can (for each group of students)
- Large empty coffee can (for each group of students)
- Large empty soup can (for each group of students)
- Electric drill or hammer and nail
- Pencil

Science Buzz

In order for bells and chimes to ring out, they must be able to vibrate freely, or *resonate*. All objects have the potential to do this, but because of their high density and uniform construction, metallic, ceramic, and glass objects tend to resonate best. Placing an object on a surface or holding it in your hands dampens the vibrations, so the sound produced is usually much more quiet and lasts for a shorter period of time.

In percussion instruments (ones that you hit to play), the pitch of the sound is controlled by both the mass (weight) and size of the object that's being hit. The heavier, more massive an object is, the deeper the sound it produces. This is because heavier objects tend to vibrate more slowly than objects that are lighter. The slower the vibrations, the lower the frequency or pitch of the sound.

Before You Start

Remove any paper or plastic labels from the cans so they are just bare metal. Use the drill (or hammer and nail) to make a small hole in the center of the bottom of each can. Make a set of Coffee Can Chimes to share with students (see page 17).

What to Do

❶ Ask students: Have you ever watched someone play a gong or triangle in an orchestra or band? Why do you think these instruments are always held up by a string or strap? *(So they can vibrate freely.)*

❷ Invite a student volunteer to be your "bell ringer." Grasp the string attached to the largest can and suspend the can in the air. Ask the bell ringer to use the pencil to gently tap the top rim of the can, and have the class listen to the sound that is produced. The can should ring out like a bell.

❸ Have students guess what will happen if you repeat the experiment but hold the can by its sides this time. Hold the can firmly in your hands by the sides and have the bell ringer strike it again. This time, the can should just have a metallic thud.

❹ Explain that in order for a bell or a gong to keep ringing, it must be able to vibrate freely, or *resonate*. Invite students to create their own Coffee Can Chimes. Photocopy and distribute "Chimes and Gongs" (p. 17) to each student.

Chimes and Gongs

Use cans of different sizes to create a set of musical chimes.

❶ Slip a piece of string through the hole in the large coffee can and tie the end to a washer inside the can. This will allow you to suspend the can by lifting the other end of the string. Repeat this procedure with the smaller coffee can and the soup can.

❷ Hold up the largest can by the string so that it hangs in the air. Gently tap the with the pencil. What does the sound remind you of?

_____

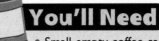

You'll Need

- Small empty coffee can with a hole drilled into the bottom
- Large empty coffee can with a hole drilled into the bottom
- Large empty soup can with a hole drilled into the bottom
- 3 12-inch pieces of string
- 3 small metal washers
- Pencil

❸ Predict: Do you think the other two cans will sound the same as the largest can? Why do you think so?

_____

_____

_____

❹ Hold up the middle-size can by the string. Gently tap the can with the pencil. How does the sound of this can compare to the large one? Why do you think this is so?

_____

_____

_____

❺ Hold up the smallest can by the string and gently tap it with the pencil. How does its sound compare with the first two?

_____

_____

_____

Think About It: What do you think controls the pitch of instruments such as bells, drums, and chimes?

Phasers and Croakers

Get It Together

- Small empty coffee can with lid (for each group of students)
- Large empty coffee can (for each group of students)
- Electric drill or hammer and a large nail
- Metal Slinky®-type spring (Note: A plastic spring will not work; if you don't have a Slinky®, any metal spring will work.)
- Pliers
- Pencil

Science Buzz

Acoustic (non-electronic) instruments, like violins and guitars, use a principle called *forced vibrations* to increase the volume of sound. Forced vibrations happen when one vibrating object is connected or "coupled" to another larger object that is also designed to vibrate. When a guitar string is plucked, for example, vibrations pass through the bridge of the guitar to the "soundboard," which is usually the top of the instrument. When the top vibrates, it also vibrates the air below it. The greater the amount of air that vibrates, the louder the sound. Most acoustic instruments have holes cut into the soundboard that are designed to let the vibrating air escape, projecting the sound outward.

Over the years sound engineers called *foley artists* have discovered that all sorts of simple devices that normally make very quiet sounds can be amplified to create very interesting sound effects. Springs have a distinctive "ricochet" sound because when they are struck at one end, the sound wave travels to the other end of the spring and back to the starting point. You actually hear the sound twice—once when it goes forward and again when it returns! The difference in timing between these two sounds is what produces the characteristic "ping," which has become a classic sound effect in modern sci-fi movies and video games.

Before You Start

Use the drill (or hammer and nail) to make a small hole in the center of the bottom of each can. Some Slinkys® have a metal tab that attaches the last coil to the rest of the spring. Remove the tab using a pair of pliers so the Slinky® can be threaded into the bottom of the coffee can.

What to Do

❶ Ask students how many have heard someone playing an acoustic (non-electrified) instrument like a cello or violin. Ask: How do these acoustic instruments make such a loud sound when they are not plugged into an amplifier? *(They all are designed to vibrate air.)*

❷ Explain that in non-electrified instruments, the trick to making them loud is to vibrate as much air as possible. The greater the volume of vibrating air, the louder the sound.

❸ Invite a student volunteer to grasp one end of the spring as you hold the other end. Stretch the spring out a little ways so that it is fairly tight. Ask students to listen and watch carefully as you tap one end of the spring with a pencil. Ask: What did you see and hear? *(The spring will vibrate but students probably won't hear much sound.)*

❹ Take one end of the spring and thread it into the hole at the bottom of a coffee can. Ask the volunteer to hold the coffee can and begin to stretch the spring out, being careful not to pull the end back out of the can. When you've stretched the spring tight, use the pencil to give it a tap. Ask: What does the spring sound like now? *(Most students will recognize the sound as a "phaser" or "blaster" sound effect.)*

❺ Explain that in the early days of radio and the movies, sound-effects specialists called *foley artists* used common objects to make very cool sounds.

❻ Invite students to make their own sound effects. Photocopy and distribute "Create a Croaker" (p. 20) to students so they can find out how simple objects can make some serious sound effects.

Create a Croaker

Use a comb and a coffee can to create a beastly sound effect!

❶ Hold a plastic comb in your hand and run your finger over its teeth. What does it sound like?

_____

_____

❷ Take the comb and hook one end of it into the hole in the small coffee can. Run your fingers over the teeth again. How does it sound this time?

_____

❸ Predict: What do you think will happen to the sound if you put the lid on the can and try the experiment again?

_____

❹ Snap the lid on the coffee can and repeat Step 2. What happens? What do you think is going on?

_____

_____

❺ Predict: What do you think will happen if you use the larger can instead of the smaller can?

_____

_____

❻ Place the comb into the hole in the bottom of the larger coffee can. Run your fingers over the teeth of the comb. What happens? What do you think is going on?

_____

_____

Think About It: How do you think acoustic instruments like cellos and violins amplify the sound of the vibrating string?

You'll Need

- Plastic pocket comb
- Small empty coffee can with hole drilled into the bottom
- Plastic lid for the small coffee can
- Large empty coffee can with hole punched in the bottom

Coffee Can Guitar

Get It Together
- Small empty coffee can (for each group of students)
- Electric drill or hammer and large nail

Science Buzz

All stringed instruments follow the same general principle: The tighter the string, the higher the pitch of the note produced. The *pitch* of a sound is controlled by the frequency of the sound wave produced. *Frequency* is defined as the number of vibrations per second. Since a tight string vibrates faster than a loose string, it has a higher frequency and a higher pitch. Many stringed instruments, like the piano and harp, have strings of different lengths that allow many notes to be played. In general, the longer the string, the slower it vibrates and the lower its pitch. In order to get a long string to vibrate at the same frequency as a short string, it must be made tighter. This can be done by either tightening the tuning peg or by placing the finger higher on the neck of the instrument, effectively shortening the string.

Before You Start

Use the drill (or hammer and nail) to make two holes, about two inches apart, in the bottom of each can. Make a model Coffee Can Guitar to share with students (see page 22).

What to Do

❶ Ask students to describe how a person plays a guitar. *(One hand plucks the string while the other hand moves up and down the neck of the guitar.)*

❷ Ask a student volunteer to come forward to assist you. Hold up the model Coffee Can Guitar and ask the class to listen carefully. Stretch the 12-inch string so it is fairly tight, then have the volunteer pluck it so it makes a sound.

❸ Next, stretch out the 18-inch string. Have students predict what the longer string will sound like compared to the first string. Will the pitch be higher, lower, or the same?

❹ Repeat step 2 with the longer string, making sure that you pull the string to about the same tension as you did with the first one. Ask students to think about what caused the difference in the two sounds.

❺ Invite students to create their own Coffee Can Guitar. Photocopy and distribute "Create a Guitar" (p. 22) to each student.

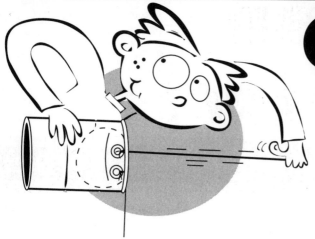

Create a Guitar

Use a coffee can and string to make a simple guitar!

❶ Slip the 12-inch string through one of the holes in the bottom of the coffee can. Tie the metal washer to the end of the string inside the can and pull it tight to make sure it doesn't slip back out of the can. Repeat with the 18-inch string.

You'll Need

- Small empty coffee can with two holes at the bottom
- 2 small metal washers
- 12-inch piece of string
- 18-inch piece of string

❷ Grasp the end of the shorter string with one hand and hold the coffee can in the other. Pull the string tight and use your thumb to pluck the string. Listen carefully to the sound it makes.

❸ Repeat Step 2 with the longer string. Which string has the lower pitch? Why do you think this is so?

_____

_____

_____

❹ Predict: What can you do to make the longer string sound the same as the shorter string? Test your prediction by trying it out. Write your results here:

_____

_____

_____

Think About It: Using the Coffee Can Guitar as a model, how do you think the different strings of a real guitar allow you to play different notes?

Coffee Can Freezer

OBJECTIVE: **To demonstrate how to freeze a liquid using a change in the physical properties of ice**

Get It Together

- Small coffee can with lid (for each group of students)
- Lab thermometer
- $\frac{1}{2}$ cup salt
- 16-oz plastic cup
- 5 or 6 ice cubes
- Plastic spoon

Science Buzz

Salt water freezes at a lower temperature than freshwater. Water normally freezes at 32°F (0°C). A 10-percent salt solution freezes at 20°F (−6.7°C) and a 20-percent salt solution freezes at 2°F (−16.7°C). When salt is added to ice, it lowers water's *freezing point* (the temperature at which liquid turns into solid) so the ice begins to melt. This is why highway departments place salt on the roads in winter to keep them from icing over.

This is also the basic principle behind old-fashioned, hand-cranked ice-cream freezers. Before electric or gas freezers were available, people would make ice cream by breaking up ice and mixing it with salt in special buckets. They would then put the cream mixture in a special container inside the bucket. Because the cream-filled container was surrounded by the salt/ice mixture, the temperature inside dropped below its freezing point, turning the cream to solid.

Before You Start

Remove any paper or plastic labels from the coffee cans. Make sure the lids fit tightly on the coffee cans and that they have no cracks or holes.

What to Do

❶ Poll the class to see who likes to eat ice cream. Explain that before there were electric freezers people had to use science and some good old-fashioned ingenuity to enjoy a frozen treat.

❷ Place a lab thermometer in a plastic cup and carefully put four or five ice cubes around the thermometer bulb. Allow the thermometer to sit in the ice for a full minute. Invite a student volunteer to come up and read the temperature. It should be close to 0°C.

❸ Ask: What do you think will happen to the temperature if we add some salt to the ice? Remove the thermometer and slowly pour in about $\frac{1}{2}$ cup of salt into the cup while stirring the ice with the spoon. DO NOT stir the the ice with the thermometer!

❹ After two minutes put the thermometer back into the mixture and allow it to sit for a full minute. Remove the thermometer and have another student volunteer read the temperature. (The temperature should read about 4 to 6 degrees below 0°C.)

❺ Invite students to use some salt, ice, and juice to make their own frozen treat. Photocopy and distribute "The Big Chill" (p. 24) to each student.

The Big Chill

Use a coffee can, some ice, and salt to make your own tasty frozen treat!

❶ Pour the fruit juice into the small plastic bag and zip it closed. Place the small bag inside the bigger bag and zip it closed too.

❷ Place four ice cubes in the empty coffee can and place the plastic bags on top of the ice. Fill the remainder of the can with ice cubes and snap the lid on tightly.

❸ Sit on the floor about three feet away from a partner. Roll the can back and forth between the two of you for two minutes. Carefully remove the lid. Observe the juice inside the bag. What changes do you see? Write your observations here:

You'll Need

- Small coffee can with lid
- Plastic spoon
- 10 ice cubes
- $\frac{1}{2}$ cup salt
- $\frac{1}{2}$ cup fruit juice
- Small plastic zipper-style bag
- Large plastic zipper-style bag
- Watch or timer
- A partner

_____

_____

_____

❹ Put the bag back into the coffee can and, if necessary, add some more ice cubes to fill the can. Pour the salt over the ice and snap the lid back on.

❺ Predict: Based on your experience with salt and ice, what do you think will happen to the juice inside the bag when you roll the can this time ?

_____

_____

❻ Roll the can back and forth between you for two full minutes. Then carefully remove the lid. Observe the juice inside the bag. What happened this time? Why do you think this is?

_____

_____

_____

Think About It: What happens to the freezing point of water when salt is added to it?

Coffee Can Science Scholastic Teaching Resources

Conduction Cans

Get It Together

- 2 small empty coffee cans (for each group of students)
- Metal pot with a plastic or wooden handle

Science Buzz

Conduction is one way that heat can be transferred from one object to another. In this process, heat energy moves through an object because as the material gets hotter on one side, the molecules vibrate faster and actually collide with adjacent cooler molecules. How well a material conducts heat depends on its atomic structure. Metals are good conductors because they have "loose" electrons in their atoms that are free to move when energized. Other materials, like wood and plastic, have electrons that are held tightly in their atomic structures so it takes a lot more energy to get them going. In this activity, students will discover that metal foil is a better conductor than plastic tape.

Conductors and insulators are used all the time to control the flow of heat. The cooking part of a pan is made of metal so that food can heat up quickly, while its handle is often made of wood or plastic to keep you from burning your hands.

Before You Start

You may prefer to conduct this experiment as a teacher demonstration rather than a hands-on activity for students. Students can complete their worksheets after they have taken turns coming to the demonstration table to collect their data.

Remove any paper or plastic labels from the coffee cans. Make a set of Conduction Cans to model for students (see page 26).

What to Do

❶ Pass a cooking pot around the room so students can feel the different materials it is made of. Ask: What are some of the differences between the pot's handle and its cooking surface? (*The material they are made of, shape, color, texture, hardness, temperature, and so on*)

❷ Tell students that different materials have different properties that make them useful for different things. Explain that cooking pots are often made of metal because metal allows heat energy to travel through it very quickly. Metals are good conductors of heat.

❸ Ask students: What do you think would happen if a pot handle was also made of metal? (*The handle would also get hot.*)

❹ Invite students to create their own Conduction Cans. Photocopy and distribute "Hot Stuff" (p. 26) to each student.

Hot Stuff

Test to see how different materials conduct heat!

❶ Wrap the outside of one coffee can with duct tape and the other with aluminum foil. The tape should be one layer thick, and there should be no spaces where the bare metal underneath shows through.

❷ Place the two coffee cans side by side on a table in front of you. Touch the outside of the two cans. Describe how they feel, including their temperature.

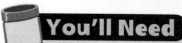

You'll Need

- 2 small empty coffee cans
- Duct tape
- Aluminum foil
- $^1/_2$ gallon or 2-liter pitcher of warm water
- Scissors

_____

_____

_____

❸ Predict: Which can do you think will feel warmer on the outside when filled with hot water? Write your prediction here:

_____

❹ Fill each can with an equal amount of hot tap water and allow them to stand for about one minute. Touch the outside of each coffee can. Which feels warmer? Why do you think this is so?

_____

_____

_____

Think About It: Why is it better for cooking pots to have wooden or plastic handles instead of metal? What other materials might work the same way as the plastic tape did?

Friction Can

Get It Together
· 1 cup (250 ml) of dry sand (for each group of students)

Science Buzz
Whenever objects rub against each other, some of the mechanical energy of motion is converted to heat energy due to friction. The greater the friction, the more heat is generated. Sometimes the heat generated by friction can be a problem. In a car engine, for example, the rubbing of metal parts against each other can cause them to heat up so much that they expand and seize the engine. To minimize the friction, lubricants, such as motor oil, are used.

Before You Begin
Allow the sand to sit out of direct sunlight and away from any heat sources (such as radiators) for about 30 minutes. This will allow the temperature of the sand to stabilize.

What to Do
❶ Have students place their hands firmly together and begin rubbing them as hard as they can. Ask: What is causing your hands to heat up? (*Friction*)

❷ Explain that friction is a *force*. (A force is a push or a pull.) Whenever two things rub together, friction transforms some of the energy of motion into heat. The greater the friction, the more heat is produced.

❸ Have students predict what would happen to the temperature of sand that is rubbed together for a few minutes.

❹ Invite students to create their own Friction Can. Photocopy and distribute "A Whole Lotta Shakin' Going On" (p. 28) to each student.

A Whole Lotta Shakin' Going On

Use a coffee can, sand, and a whole lotta shakin' to generate some heat!

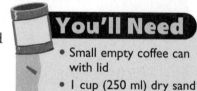

You'll Need

- Small empty coffee can with lid
- 1 cup (250 ml) dry sand
- Lab thermometer
- Watch or timer

1 Pour the sand into the coffee can. Insert the thermometer into the sand so that the bulb is completely covered.

2 Allow the thermometer to stand for one full minute. Remove the thermometer and read the temperature. Record the starting temperature of the sand below:

Starting Temperature of Sand: _____ degrees C

3 Place the thermometer aside in a safe location and snap the lid onto the can tightly.

4 Predict: What will happen to the temperature of the sand after you shake the can for five minutes?

_____

_____

5 Begin shaking the can as vigorously as possible, keeping one hand on the lid so that it doesn't come off. Shake the can for a full five minutes without stopping. You and your classmates may want to take turns shaking the can.

6 After five minutes, stop shaking the can and place it on a table. Remove the lid and place the thermometer bulb into the sand. Let the thermometer stand for one minute and then remove it and read the temperature. Record the ending temperature of the sand below:

Ending Temperature of Sand: _____ degrees C

7 What happened to the temperature of the sand after you shook it in the coffee can? Why do you think this is?

_____

_____

_____

Think About It: Why do you think moving objects often heat up?

Friction Cans II

Get It Together
- 10- by 24-inch wooden board
- Small empty coffee can with two plastic lids (for each group of students)
- Water
- 3 thick textbooks or wooden blocks

Science Buzz

Any time an object here on Earth moves, it experiences some friction. *Friction* is a force that works to slow moving objects as they rub against things around them. Friction is caused by irregularities (rough spots) along the surface of a material. The amount of friction depends on the types of material that are moving against each other, how rough they are, and how hard they are pressing together.

While friction is usually associated with external surfaces, there is also internal friction. A rolling coffee can partially filled with different materials will experience internal friction as the material inside rubs against the inside of the can. A can half-filled with water will roll slowly down a ramp, while a can half-filled with sand is almost impossible to roll. If the same can is completely filled with sand, however, it will roll easily because the sand inside will have very little room to move, so it behaves as one solid mass. The sand is not rubbing on the inside of the cans, so there's minimal internal friction to slow down the can.

Before You Start

Make sure that you have the use of a long, straight hallway or a clear path in your classroom that is at least 15 feet long. Set up the ramp: Prop the wooden board on a stack of textbooks.

What to Do

❶ Have students rub their hands together. Ask: What force is causing your hands to get warm? *(Friction)*

❷ Explain that friction is a force that works against moving things as they rub against each other. Friction doesn't always have to work on the outside of objects, however. Sometimes it can be on the inside, too.

❸ Take an empty coffee can and snap a lid on both its top and bottom. Ask students to predict what will happen when you place the can at the top of the ramp and let it go. *(The empty can will roll down the ramp and continue for a few feet.)*

❹ Take the same can and fill it with a cup of water. Ask students to predict what will happen when you roll it down the ramp this time. *(The can will roll down the ramp but will not travel as far as the empty can.)*

❺ Explain that as the can is rolling, the water rubs against the inside of the can. This creates friction, which slows down the can.

❻ Invite students to conduct their own friction experiments. Photocopy and distribute "The Big Rub" (p. 30) to each student.

The Big Rub

Use rolling coffee cans to discover how friction works to slow things down!

❶ Snap a lid on each end of the coffee can. Lay the can on its side at the top of the ramp and let it go.

❷ Use a piece of masking tape to mark where the empty can stopped rolling. Measure the distance from the bottom of the ramp to the tape and record it under "Actual Distance Rolled" in the first row of the chart below.

You'll Need
- Small empty coffee can
- 2 plastic coffee can lids
- Dry sand
- Ramp
- Masking tape
- Yardstick or meter stick

Coffee Can	Predicted Distance	Actual Distance Rolled
Empty		
Filled with sand		
Half-filled with sand		

❸ Retrieve the coffee can and open one lid. Fill the can with sand, making sure there is almost no empty space inside. Snap the lid back on tightly. Predict: How far do you think the can will roll this time? Record your prediction on the chart in the row labeled "Filled with sand."

❹ Place the can at the top of the ramp and let it go. Repeat Step 2, recording your result in the second row.

❺ Retrieve the coffee can and carefully open one lid. Pour out about half of the sand so the can is only half full. Snap the lid back on tightly. Predict: How far do you think the can will roll this time? Record your prediction in the row labeled "Half-filled with sand."

❻ Place the can at the top of the ramp and let it go. Repeat Step 2, recording your result in the bottom row.

Think About It: How does friction inside the can affect its ability to roll?

Potential Energy Can

Get It Together

- 10- by 24-inch wooden board
- 3 thick textbooks or wooden blocks
- Small empty coffee can (for each group of students)
- Can opener
- Small, bouncy ball

Science Buzz

Potential energy is energy that is stored and can be used to do work. Whenever an object is lifted off a surface, it gains *gravitational potential energy*. (*Gravity* is the force that pulls objects toward the earth.) The higher you lift an object, the greater the amount of stored energy and the greater its potential to do work (or damage). When an object rolls down a ramp, its potential energy is transformed into *kinetic energy*, the energy of motion. If the height of a ramp is increased, the gravitational potential energy of the object at the top of the ramp is also increased. An object rolling down a steep ramp has more kinetic energy and usually rolls a greater distance than the same object placed on a low ramp.

Gravitational potential energy is used to get work done in many different ways. Perhaps the most fun use of gravitational potential energy is in roller coasters. Once a roller coaster reaches the top of the first hill, gravity keeps it going the rest of the way!

Before You Start

Make sure that you have the use of a long, straight hallway or a clear path in your classroom that is at least 15 feet long. Set up the ramp: Prop the wooden board on one thick textbook or wooden block. Put extra textbooks next to the ramp.

Use a can opener to remove both ends of the coffee cans so they are hollow cylinders.

What to Do

❶ Ask students: What is gravity? (*The force that holds us down to the earth's surface*)

❷ Ask: Can gravity get something moving? (*Yes*) After students have expressed their ideas, tell them to "follow the bouncing ball!" Ask a student volunteer to hold the ball about one foot above a table where everyone can see. Ask the student to drop the ball.

❸ Ask: What force made the ball fall? (*Gravity*) Have students predict what would happen to the ball if the volunteer drops it from a greater height. Then have your assistant hold the ball about three feet above the table and drop it. Ask: Did the ball bounce higher or lower than the first time? (*The ball should bounce higher.*)

❹ Explain that the ball bounced higher the second time because it had more energy when it hit the tabletop. Ask students to think about where this extra energy came from.

❺ Invite students to create their own Energy Cans. Photocopy and distribute "Rolling Along" (p. 32) to each student.

Rolling Along

Discover how a change in elevation really gets things rolling!

❶ Snap a lid on each end of the coffee can. Lay the can on its side at the top of the ramp and let it go.

❷ Use a piece of masking tape to mark where the can stopped. Measure the distance from the bottom of the ramp to the tape and record it under "Actual Distance Rolled" in the first row of the chart below.

You'll Need

- Small empty coffee can with both ends removed
- 2 plastic coffee can lids
- Ramp
- Textbooks or wooden blocks
- Masking tape
- Yardstick or meter stick

Coffee Can	Predicted Distance	Actual Distance Rolled
Trial #1		
Trial #2		

❸ Place two more books or blocks under the ramp to raise it higher. Predict: What do you think will happen to the coffee can this time when you let it go? Record your prediction in the chart in the row for "Trial #2."

❹ Place the can on its side at the top of the ramp again and let it go. Repeat Step 2, recording your result in the bottom row.

Think About It: How does increasing the height of the ramp affect the amount of energy that an object rolling down it has? Where does this energy come from?

Coffee Can Science Scholastic Teaching Resources

Inertia Can

Get It Together
- 3 empty coffee cans with lids
- Large sheet of newspaper

Science Buzz
Inertia is the resistance of an object to change its motion. In other words, an object at rest will stay at rest and an object in motion will stay in motion unless some other force acts on it. The amount of inertia an object has depends on how much mass it has. The more mass an object has, the greater its inertia. It's much more difficult to push a big truck than a little car, but once the truck gets going, it's much harder to stop it.

In this activity, inertia plays only a small part in what's going on. There is also the force of friction and something called *impulse*. Even though the bottom of the coffee can and the newspaper are fairly smooth, they still rub against each other because of friction. To overcome friction between the two, you have to pull the paper fast. If you pull the paper slowly, the can will just go along for a ride because friction keeps it on the paper. By pulling the paper fast, you're creating a large impulse. *Impulse* is a measure of how fast a force acts upon something. A large impulse means that the force acts very quickly, while a small impulse means that the force acts over a long period of time.

Before You Start
You may want to practice the "magic trick" described below before doing it in front of an audience (your class). This way, you'll have a better sense of the amount of force you need to apply on the newspaper.

What to Do
❶ Tell the class that you're going to recreate a famous magic trick. Find out how many students have seen a magician place a pile of dishes on top of a tablecloth, and then pull the cloth out from underneath without moving a single plate. Ask: Is this really magic or is it science? *(Science)*

❷ Spread a sheet of newspaper on a smooth tabletop and stack three coffee cans in the shape of a pyramid on top of the paper. Grasp the edge of the newspaper and quickly pull it out from under the coffee cans. The cans should stay in place.

❸ Ask: What kept the coffee cans from falling when I pulled out the newspaper? *(The weight of the cans and the speed at which you pulled the paper)*

❹ Have students predict what would happen to the cans if you repeat the trick, this time pulling the paper slowly. After they make their predictions, try it. Explain that the speed at which you pull the paper is only part of the trick. The other part has something to do with *inertia*—an object's resistance to change in its motion.

❺ Invite students to try out some magic. Photocopy and distribute "Coffee Can Magic" (p. 34) to each student.

Coffee Can Magic

Use a coffee can and a sheet of newspaper to discover the science behind a famous magic trick!

❶ Spread the newspaper on a smooth, flat desk. Fill the coffee can halfway with pebbles or sand, and snap on the lid. Set the can in the middle of the paper and grasp the paper by the edge.

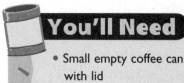

You'll Need

- Small empty coffee can with lid
- Dry sand or small pebbles
- Large sheet of newspaper
- Smooth, flat desk

❷ Slowly pull the paper toward you, making sure that the can doesn't fall on the floor. What happens? What do you think is going on?

_____

_____

❸ Return the coffee can to its starting point. Predict: What will happen if you pull the paper quickly this time?

_____

❹ Grasp the edges of the newspaper and pull it straight toward you as quickly as possible. What happens? What do you think is going on?

_____

_____

❺ Put the paper back on the table. Empty out the coffee can and put it on top of the newspaper. Predict: What will happen when you pull the paper out from under the empty coffee can?

_____

❻ Grasp the edges of the newspaper and pull it quickly straight toward you. What happens this time? How is it different from when you did it with the full coffee can? What do you think is going on?

_____

_____

Think About It: Why do you think magicians stack heavy objects on top of the tablecloth before they pull on it?

Magnetic Measurement Can

OBJECTIVE: To show that magnets have a force field surrounding them and to demonstrate how the strength of the magnetic field varies with the magnet

Get It Together
- Small empty coffee can
  (for each group of students)
- Can opener
- Different magnets

Science Buzz

All magnets, regardless of size and shape, have a magnetic field surrounding them. Even though some magnetic fields are quite strong, magnets are limited in what they can attract. Magnets attract iron, steel, and cobalt, as well as *alloys* (mixtures of metals) that contain one or more of these three metals. Since coffee cans are made out of steel, they are easily attracted to any magnet.

Coffee cans are fairly sensitive magnetic-field detectors because they roll so easily. By resetting the can to the same position at the start of each trial in this experiment, students are doing a "controlled" experiment. The only variable that changes with each trial is the magnet being used. All other conditions remain the same.

Before You Start

Use a can opener to remove the tops and bottoms from the coffee cans. Test all the magnets to make sure that they are strong enough to attract the coffee cans. If magnets are in short supply, ask students to bring in magnets from home to test out.

What to Do

❶ Tell students that you're going to hold a little investigation with magnets. Have students predict what will happen when you touch a magnet to a coffee can. Bring the magnet in contact with the side of the coffee can. Ask: Why is the coffee can attracted to the magnet? *(The can is made of steel.)*

❷ Ask: Do you think the magnet has to actually touch the coffee can to be attracted to it? Allow students to offer their opinions. Take a coffee can and lay it on its side on a desk. Take the strongest magnet that you have and bring it close to the side of the can without touching it. The can will start to roll in the direction of the magnet, proving that a magnet need only get near an object in order to attract it.

❸ Explain that all magnets have an area around them where they can pull or push on other magnetic materials. This space is called the *magnetic field*, and even though it's invisible, it can be measured. The stronger a magnet, the farther the magnetic field reaches into space.

❹ Demonstrate for students how to set up their own magnetic-field test can, then invite them to conduct their own experiments. Photocopy and distribute "Magnetic Moments" (p. 36) to each student.

Magnetic Moments

Use a coffee can to test the strength of different magnets.

❶ Use the marker and a piece of masking tape to label the magnets A, B, C, and D.

❷ Predict: After looking at the magnets, which one do you think has the strongest magnetic field? Why do you think so?

_____

_____

_____

You'll Need

• Small empty coffee can with both ends removed
• Masking tape
• Pencil or marker
• 4 different magnets
• White copier paper

❸ Place a piece of plain white paper flat on the desk and tape the four corners to hold the paper in place. Lay the coffee can on its side at the left-hand, shorter edge of the paper, as shown.

❹ Take magnet A and place it at the opposite end of the paper, across from the coffee can. Slowly slide the magnet across the paper toward the coffee can. As soon as the coffee can starts to roll toward the magnet, stop moving the magnet. Mark this point on the paper with a pencil and write the magnet's letter next to the mark.

❺ Set the coffee can back at its starting point. Repeat Step 4 three more times, using magnets B, C, and D.

❻ Which magnet has the strongest magnetic field? How do you know?

_____

_____

_____

Think About It: Do the magnetic fields of all magnets have the same strength? Besides coffee cans, what other materials could you use to test the strength of magnetic fields?

Electric Coffee Can

OBJECTIVE: To show that static electricity can be used to charge metallic objects

Get It Together

- Small coffee can (for each group of students)
- Piece of wool or wool sock
- Can opener
- 12-inch round balloon

Science Buzz

Static electricity results from electrons accumulating on the surface of an object. Because of their atomic structure, some materials, like rubber, wax, and amber, are *electron acceptors* (they grab onto free electrons), while others, like wool and hair, are *electron donors* (they lose free electrons).

In this activity, the rubber balloon collects and stores electrons from different types of materials. Once the balloon is charged and brought near the steel coffee can, it induces a charge on the can. Charging by induction happens easily in metals because they are good electrical conductors. When the charged balloon is brought near the surface of the coffee can, it forces away electrons on the near side of the can. (Remember, like charges repel each other.) This leaves the near side of the can with a positive charge. Since opposite charges attract, the can rolls toward the balloon. The greater the static charge on the balloon surface, the faster the can will roll.

Before You Start

Use a can opener to remove the tops and bottoms from the coffee cans. Have extra balloons to replace any that break during the activity. This activity is best conducted on a cool, dry day when humidity is low.

What to Do

❶ Invite a student volunteer to assist you with a demonstration. Select a student with long hair without any mousse or hair spray in it. Tell your volunteer that you're going to see if she has a "head for science."

❷ Inflate one of the balloons and knot it. Rub the balloon a few times across the student's hair and slowly lift it off. The hair should be attracted to the balloon. Ask students: What do you think is causing this hair-raising effect? *(Static electricity)*

❸ Lay a coffee can on its side on a flat surface in front of the room, where students can see it. Take the inflated balloon and rub it with the piece of wool. Explain that by rubbing the balloon, you are charging it with static electricity. Bring the charged balloon near the coffee can. The can should start to roll toward it.

❹ Explain that wool is a material that generates a great deal of static. Ask: Do you think all materials generate the same amount of static? Invite students to test the items around them for static. Photocopy and distribute "Coffee Can Electroscope" (p. 38) to each student.

Coffee Can Electroscope

Use an "electric" coffee can and a balloon to test the static potential of different materials.

❶ Lay the coffee can on its side on a flat surface in front of you. Inflate the balloon and tie a knot in it.

❷ Rub the balloon on your hair a few times and then bring it close to the coffee can WITHOUT ACTUALLY TOUCHING IT. What happens? What do you think is going on?

_____

_____

_____

You'll Need

- Small coffee can with top and bottom removed
- 12-inch round balloon
- Hardcover textbook
- Small piece of aluminum foil
- Small piece of wax paper
- Small piece of plastic wrap

❸ Touch the balloon to the coffee can to discharge any static electricity. Test the other materials to see if they can get the coffee can to move. On each trial, rub the balloon several times across the material and then bring it near the coffee can to see how well it is attracted to the charged balloon. Check the correct column for each material in the chart below. After each test, touch the balloon to the coffee can to discharge any static electricity.

Material	Strong Attraction	Weak Attraction	No Attraction
Textbook			
Aluminum foil			
Wax paper			
Plastic wrap			
Your shirt			
Your pants or skirt			

Think About It: Based on your experiment, what can you say about the ability of different materials to generate static electricity? Which types of materials seem to generate the most static?

Coffee Can Science Scholastic Teaching Resources

Energy Transfer Can

OBJECTIVE: To demonstrate how potential and kinetic energy can be exchanged for each other

Get It Together

- Small empty coffee can (for each group of students)
- Pointy scissors
- Can opener
- 2 coffee-can lids (for each can)
- Large rubber band

Science Buzz

Energy makes things move. There are many different forms of energy but they all can be grouped into two broad categories: *kinetic energy*, which is the energy of motion, and *potential energy*, which is energy that is stored and waiting to be used.

In this activity, these two forms of energy transfer back and forth between each other. Here's how it works: As the can rolls, the weight (metal nut) causes the rubber band to wind up inside the can. As it does, the kinetic energy of the rolling can is stored in the rubber band as potential energy. By the time the can stops, much of the kinetic energy has turned into stored potential energy in the rubber band. When the rubber band begins to unwind itself, some of this potential energy is converted back into kinetic energy. The can eventually comes to a halt because much of the energy is used to overcome friction.

In mechanical devices, potential and kinetic energy are exchanged for each other all the time. One example is in an old-fashioned clock. When you wind up the spring, you are using the kinetic energy to store potential energy in the spring. As the spring unwinds, the stored potential energy is turned back into kinetic energy to make the hands of the clock move.

Before You Start

Use a can opener to remove the tops and bottoms from the coffee cans. Use the pointy scissors to punch two holes, about $\frac{1}{2}$ inch (1.25 cm) apart, in each lid. Make sure the holes are evenly spaced on either side of the center of the lid. Make a model Energy Transfer Can to share with students (see page 40).

What to Do

❶ Stretch a long rubber band between your fingers and then let it go as if you were shooting it into the air. Be careful to aim away from students! Ask: Why did the rubber band fly when I let it go? (*Because you stretched the rubber band.*)

❷ Have students predict what would happen if you tried to "shoot" the rubber band again without stretching it first. (*The rubber band would just fall to the floor.*)

❸ Explain that when you stretch the rubber band, you are giving it *potential energy*—energy that is stored and waiting to be used. When you let the rubber band go, the stored potential energy turns into *kinetic energy*, the energy of motion.

❹ Show students the model Energy Transfer Can. Place it on the floor and give it a push so it starts rolling. When it stops, shout, "Come back!" The can will slowly roll back to where it started. Have students guess what is going on inside the can to get it to move back.

❺ Invite students to create their own Energy Transfer Can. Photocopy and distribute "Create an Energy Transfer Can" (p. 40) to each student.

Create an Energy Transfer Can

Use a coffee can and a rubber band to create a clever little toy!

You'll Need
- Small empty coffee can with both ends removed
- 2 coffee-can lids with 2 holes punched in each lid
- Long, thin rubber band that has been cut
- 2-oz fishing weight or a heavy metal nut
- Short string

❶ Take the two coffee-can lids and hold them together so that the bottom sides are facing each other. Carefully thread a rubber band through the two holes in one lid, then through the holes of the other lid. Knot the ends of the rubber band tightly.

❷ Place the fishing weight or metal nut between the two lids and tie it to the rubber band, as shown.

❸ Bend one lid and slip it through the metal cylinder so you can place it on the other end of the can. Place the other lid on the other end. Be careful not to tangle the rubber band.

❹ Test your Energy Transfer Can by laying it on its side and rolling it across a smooth floor. It should roll a few feet, stop, and then roll back toward you. If it does not work, make sure the fishing weight or metal nut is hanging freely from the rubber band inside the can.

❺ What do you think is happening to the rubber band when you roll the can forward? Draw what you think the rubber band looks like and label your drawing:

❻ What do you think is happening to the rubber band when the can stops and begins to roll backward? Draw what you think the rubber band looks like and label your drawing:

❼ What do you think is the purpose of the heavy weight attached to the rubber band?

_____

_____

Think About It: How do you think potential energy and kinetic energy are being transferred in the Energy Transfer Can?

Coffee Can Science Scholastic Teaching Resources

Mechanical Weathering Can

Get It Together
- Small empty coffee can (for each group of students)
- 4 different rock specimens, each about 1 inch (2 cm) across (for each group of students)
- Small cup of sand
- Newspaper
- Large rock sample
- Hammer
- Safety goggles

Science Buzz

All rocks wear down over time through a process called *weathering*. *Physical* or *mechanical weathering* occurs when rocks split and break due to temperature changes, ice, or simply banging together. Some rocks are more resistant to weathering than others. Hard minerals, like quartz and feldspar, can take a great deal of punishment, while soft minerals, like talc and mica, can be easily worn away.

The way minerals are joined together in a rock is another important factor in determining how resistant a rock is to weathering. Sedimentary rocks, like sandstone and limestone, tend to wear down easily because they are composed of individual mineral grains that have been cemented or compacted together. In igneous rocks, like granite, the minerals are fused together because they crystallized from molten rock.

Before You Start

Wash all the rock specimens and the inside of the coffee cans. Make sure the plastic lids fit tightly on the coffee cans.

What to Do

❶ Introduce the activity by passing around a cup of sand. Invite students to examine the sand closely. Ask: What is sand? (*Small broken fragments of rocks*)

❷ Spread newspaper on a desk or table where students can see, and invite a volunteer to assist you. Place the large rock sample on the paper and give the volunteer safety glasses. Have the volunteer use the hammer to gently hit the rock a few times. Ask: What are we making when we hit the rock with the hammer? (*Sand*)

❸ Explain that in the real world, most sand doesn't come from people pounding on rocks with hammers. Instead, sand is created naturally through a process called *mechanical weathering*. Have students think about how sand gets created in the natural environment. Ask: Do you think all rocks weather the same way? (*No*)

❹ Invite students to put some rocks to the test. Photocopy and distribute "Rock and Roll" (p. 42) to each student.

Rock and Roll

Use a coffee can to test and see how resistant different rocks are to weathering.

You'll Need
- Small empty coffee can with lid
- 4 different clean rock specimens, each about 1 inch (2 cm) across
- Penny
- 12-oz clear plastic cup
- Water
- Watch or timer

❶ Examine the four rock samples closely. Do they all look and feel the same? Describe the four samples here:

_____

_____

_____

_____

❷ Use your fingernail to try to scratch each rock sample. Then, use a penny to do the same thing. Are all the rocks the same hardness? Rank the four samples from hardest to softest by putting letters next to their descriptions. Label the hardest sample "A" and the softest sample "D."

❸ Put the rocks in the coffee can and pour in a cup of clean water. Predict: What do you think will happen to the rocks after you shake the can for a few minutes? Will all the rocks behave in the same way?

_____

_____

❹ Snap the lid on tightly and shake the can as hard as you can for five minutes. Make sure to keep the lid pointed up to avoid water leaks! You and your classmates may want to take turns shaking the can.

❺ After five minutes, carefully remove the lid and pour the water back into the plastic cup. Remove the four rocks and examine each one closely. How have they changed? Have they all changed in the same way?

_____

_____

Think About It: What is the relationship between the hardness of a rock and the rate at which it weathers? What would be some ideal places to look for sand forming naturally from rocks?

Coffee Can Science Scholastic Teaching Resources

Frost Wedging Can

Get It Together
- 2 ice cubes
- 2 rock samples each about 3 cm (1 inch) across
- 2 clear 16-oz plastic tumblers half-filled with water
- Plastic zipper-style sandwich bag

Science Buzz

When water turns solid, it expands 9 percent by volume. While this doesn't sound like much, the force exerted by expanding ice not only can shatter glass bottles left in a freezer, it can also split solid rock. In areas with warm days and cold nights, *frost wedging* is one of the chief forms of mechanical weathering. Ice splits up rocks into smaller pieces, giving water and other chemicals a chance to wear down rocks even further.

Before You Start

This activity is best done either as a demonstration or as a take-home activity. If you are going to do it in school, make sure that you have the use of a freezer.

What to Do

❶ Pass around an ice cube in a sealed sandwich bag and one of the rock samples. Ask students to compare the two and list some of their similarities. *(Both are solid, nonliving or inorganic, hard, and so on.)*

❷ Explain to students that based on a geologic definition, an ice cube is really a mineral, just like the stuff that makes up rocks. There are a few important differences between ice and other minerals, however.

❸ Hold up a plastic tumbler filled with water. Have students predict what will happen when you place the rock in the water. *(The rock should sink unless it's pumice.)* Place the rock into the water and show it sinking to the bottom of the tumbler.

❹ Hold up the other tumbler of water and ask students to predict what will happen when you put an ice cube in it. *(The ice will float on the water.)* Place the ice into the water and show students that it floats.

❺ Explain that when water turns to ice, its *density*—the amount of matter per unit volume—decreases. That's why ice always floats on water. When water freezes, this change in density can have a serious impact on other rocks and minerals through a process called *frost wedging*.

❻ Photocopy and distribute "The Big Freeze" (p. 44) to help students learn more about frost wedging.

The Big Freeze

Use a coffee can and a freezer to see how frost wedging happens in rocks!

❶ Fill the empty coffee can to the top with water and snap the lid on tight. To further secure the lid, wrap the two rubber bands around the top and bottom of the can in a crisscross fashion.

You'll Need
- Small empty coffee can with lid
- Water
- 2 large, thick rubber bands
- Freezer

❷ Place the coffee can full of water in the freezer. Predict: What will happen to the water as it changes from liquid to solid?

_____

_____

_____

❸ Allow the can to sit in the freezer undisturbed for at least 12 hours.

❹ After 12 hours, remove the coffee can from the freezer. What happened to the lid? Why do you think this happened?

_____

_____

_____

_____

Think About It: What do you think will happen to a rock if water seeps inside a crack and then freezes?

Coffee Can Science Scholastic Teaching Resources

Coffee Can Barometer

Get It Together
- Clean toilet plunger or suction cup
- Aneroid barometer (optional)

Science Buzz

The earth's atmosphere is like an "ocean of air" pressing down on us from all directions. *Atmospheric pressure* is always changing. These changes in air pressure bring about changes in the weather. To keep track of changing air pressure, scientists use a device called a *barometer*—an airtight box with a measuring device hooked up to one end. As the outside air pressure changes, the pointer on the barometer either rises or falls. A rising barometer (high pressure) usually means fair weather is on the way. A falling barometer (low pressure) usually means that a storm is approaching.

Several factors influence atmospheric pressure, including temperature. When air gets warm, it expands and becomes less dense, leading to areas of low pressure. Cold air is usually dense, meaning it exerts a high pressure on the surface. Because the earth is always turning, individual "air masses" of differing pressures move around the planet, creating wind and producing storms.

Before You Start

Make a model Coffee Can Barometer to share with students (see page 46).

What to Do

❶ Take a suction cup (or toilet plunger) and press it down firmly on a smooth desk or tabletop. Ask a student volunteer to come up and remove it. When the volunteer tries to pull up, the suction cup will stick to the surface. Ask: What's making the suction cup (or plunger) stick? *(Suction)*

❷ Explain that even though it looks like the suction cup is sucking on to the surface, it's really not. The suction cup starts off with air on top and air underneath. When you press down on the cup, you squeeze out the air underneath and the air on top presses down on it. Scientists call this air pressing down *atmospheric* or *barometric pressure*.

❸ Ask: What kinds of information does a weather forecast tell you? *(Temperature, humidity, wind direction and speed, barometric pressure)* Explain that barometric pressure measures how hard the air is pressing on the surface of the earth. A change in air pressure is a sure sign of a change in the weather. Scientists use a device called a *barometer* to measure changes in air pressure.

❹ Show students your Coffee Can Barometer. Explain that a barometer is an airtight box with a measuring device hooked up to one end. Have students predict what will happen to the straw when the air pressure on either side of the balloon changes.

❺ Invite students to create their own Coffee Can Barometer. Photocopy and distribute "Build a Barometer" (p. 46) to each student.

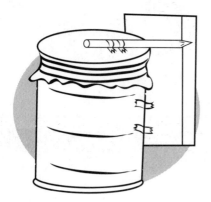

Build a Barometer

Use a coffee can, a balloon, and a plastic straw to build your own working barometer.

❶ Cut off the open end of the balloon. Stretch the large piece of rubber over the can opening so that it is tight like a drum. Wrap two rubber bands around the balloon and rim of the coffee can to make an airtight seal.

❷ Cut one end of the straw to make it look like a pointer. Tape the straight end of the straw to the middle of the balloon on top of the can. The pointy end should extend over the edge of the can.

❸ Tape the index card to the back of the coffee can, as shown. Make sure the card sticks out to the point of the straw. Use a pencil to mark where the pointer is on the card.

You'll Need

- Small empty coffee can
- 12-inch round balloon
- 2 thick rubber bands
- Plastic drinking straw
- 5- by 7-inch white index card
- Cellophane tape
- Scissors

❹ Predict: What will happen to the pointer on the barometer if outside air pressure increases and pushes down on the balloon? Why?

_____

_____

❺ Predict: What will happen to the pointer on the barometer if outside air pressure goes down? Why?

_____

_____

❻ Keep track of the changes in barometric pressure according to local weather reports over the next few days. On those same days, observe the pointer on your Coffee Can Barometer and compare your results with the weather forecast. Fill in the chart below:

	Weather Forecast (check one)	Coffee Can Barometer (check one)
Day 1	Rising _____ Falling _____	Rising _____ Falling _____
Day 2	Rising _____ Falling _____	Rising _____ Falling _____
Day 3	Rising _____ Falling _____	Rising _____ Falling _____
Day 4	Rising _____ Falling _____	Rising _____ Falling _____
Day 5	Rising _____ Falling _____	Rising _____ Falling _____

Think About It: What do you think scientists mean by rising and falling barometer?

Coffee Can Science Scholastic Teaching Resources

Dew Point Can

Get It Together
- Small empty coffee can (for each group of students)
- Lab thermometer (for each group of students)
- Glass of ice water
- Food coloring
- Paper towels

Science Buzz
One of the key indicators used in predicting the weather is the *dew point*—the temperature at which water vapor in the air will condense into liquid. The higher the dew point, the higher the relative humidity of the air and the greater the chance of rain. *Air temperature* also controls relative humidity because warm air can hold more water vapor than cold air. At night, surfaces like grass or metal railings will actually be colder than the air itself, so water condenses directly on these surfaces forming a layer called *dew*.

Before You Start
Remove any paper or plastic labels from the coffee cans so they are bare metal. Place the thermometers in the room at least 15 minutes before the activity so they can adjust to the current room temperature.

What to Do
❶ Hold up an ice-cold glass of water and add a few drops of food coloring in the water. Ask students if they've ever seen a glass "cry." Dry the outside of the glass with a paper towel. Lay a second paper towel flat on a desk or tabletop and set the glass of water on top of it. Tell students to watch the glass carefully.

❷ After about a minute or so, remove the glass and lift the paper towel to show everyone. There should be a ring of water on the towel where the glass was. Ask students: Where did the wet ring on the paper towel come from? *(The glass)* Guide students to notice that the water ring on the paper towel is colorless even though the water inside the glass is colored. That means the water didn't come from inside the glass.

❸ Explain that the water outside the glass and on the towel isn't tears, but dew. Ask students if they've ever seen tiny water drops on grass, cars, and other surfaces early in the morning. Explain that those water drops are dew. Dew forms because of *condensation*, which happens when water vapor (a gas) in the air turns into a liquid. Tell students that the temperature at which water vapor turns into liquid is called the *dew point*.

❹ Invite students to conduct their own experiment to calculate the dew point. Photocopy and distribute "Do the Dew" (p. 48) to each student.

Do the Dew

Calculate the current dew point using a coffee can and a thermometer.

❶ Read the thermometer and record the current air temperature in the room.

Room Air Temperature: _____ degrees C

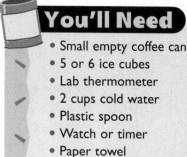

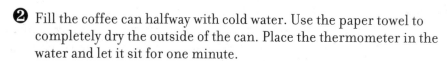
You'll Need
- Small empty coffee can
- 5 or 6 ice cubes
- Lab thermometer
- 2 cups cold water
- Plastic spoon
- Watch or timer
- Paper towel

❷ Fill the coffee can halfway with cold water. Use the paper towel to completely dry the outside of the can. Place the thermometer in the water and let it sit for one minute.

❸ Add three ice cubes to the water and gently stir with the spoon. DO NOT stir with the thermometer! Also, try not to splash water on the outside of the can. Predict: What will happen to the water temperature as the ice melts?

_____

_____

❹ Check the temperature of the thermometer every 30 seconds while you observe the outside of the can. As soon as the outside of the coffee can begins to get damp or foggy, record the temperature of the water.

Dew Point: _____ degrees C

This is the approximate dew point. (NOTE: If the ice melts before the outside of the can gets damp, add more ice to the water to lower the temperature further.)

❺ Why do you think the outside of the can gets wet as the water temperature inside the can decreases?

_____

_____

❻ Subtract the dew point (4) from the air temperature (1). The difference is how much the air in the room would have to cool before the water vapor in the air begins to condense.

_____ degrees C – _____ degrees C = _____ degrees C
   (1)   (4)

Think About It: How might you use the dew point temperature and the air temperature to predict the chance of rain?

Coffee Can Science Scholastic Teaching Resources

Albedo Cans

Get It Together
- 2 small coffee cans with lids (for each group of students)
- 2 lab thermometers (for each group of students)
- Flat black paint
- Gloss white paint
- 2 paintbrushes

Science Buzz

Albedo is a measure of how much light energy is reflected off an object and how much is absorbed and transformed into heat energy. Light-colored or shiny objects have a high albedo and reflect a large percentage of light. As a result, they don't heat up as quickly as dull, dark-colored objects. Albedo plays an important role in determining how fast the earth's surface is heated by the sun. Dark-colored rocks, roofing tar, and asphalt pavement (all of which have low albedos) heat up very quickly. This is one of the reasons that cities tend to be warmer than the surrounding countryside. Snow and ice have exceptionally high albedos, so they reflect much of the incoming sunlight. This is why snow packs and glaciers take a long time to melt.

Before You Start

Remove any paper or plastic labels from the coffee cans so they are bare metal. Paint the outside of one coffee can and lid flat black and the other can and lid gloss white. Make sure that the thermometers fit inside the coffee cans with their lids on. If the thermometers are too tall, cut a slot in each lid to allow them to slip through.

This activity is best conducted outdoors on a bright, sunny day, although it can also be conducted indoors next to a window that gets direct sunlight.

What to Do

❶ Ask students how many have heard that it's better to wear light-colored clothes than dark-colored clothes during the summer. Then ask if anyone can explain why. (*Dark colors heat up more than light colors.*)

❷ Pass around one black and one white coffee can. Have students compare the way they look and feel and note any differences. Does the black can "feel" any different from the white can? (*Not really*)

❸ Explain that the two cans are identical except for their colors. While the cans may not feel any different in the room, they react differently when they are placed under direct sunlight.

❹ Tell students that they are going to test the albedo effect. Have students predict what will happen to the two cans when they are placed in the sunlight. Photocopy and distribute "The Heat Is On" (p. 50) to each student.

The Heat Is On

Use different-colored coffee cans to test the albedo effect.

You'll Need

- Small coffee can with lid, painted black
- Small coffee can with lid, painted white
- 2 lab thermometers
- Dry sand
- Measuring cup or graduated beaker
- Watch or timer
- A sunny windowsill or access to outdoors

❶ Use the measuring cup to fill each coffee can about halfway with sand. Make sure that you put exactly the same amount of sand in each can.

❷ Place a thermometer in each can, making sure that the base of the thermometer is touching the bottom of the can. Allow the thermometers to sit in the sand for one full minute.

❸ Read the temperature on the two thermometers. They should be equal. Record the starting temperature in the chart below.

Coffee Can	Starting Temperature	End Temperature
Black Paint		
White Paint		

❹ Carefully snap the matching colored lid on each can and place the cans side by side under direct sunlight. Predict: What do you think will happen to the sand's temperature in the two cans as they sit in the sun? Why?

_____

_____

❺ Let both cans sit under direct sunlight for exactly five minutes. When time is up, take the cans out of the sun and carefully remove the lids. Immediately read the temperature on the two thermometers and record them on the chart.

❻ What happened to the temperature of the sand inside the two cans? Are they both the same?

_____

_____

Think About It: How do you think the albedo effect works for objects of different colors?

Coffee Can Science Scholastic Teaching Resources

Specific Heat Cans

Get It Together
- 2 small empty coffee cans (for each group of students)
- Flat black paint
- Paintbrush
- Cup of water
- Cup of sand

Science Buzz

Different materials heat up and store heat at different rates. While this is based partially on how well the material conducts heat, there is another factor at play. Scientists call this property *specific heat*. Of all the substances found on earth, water has one of the highest specific heats. Water can store more heat per gram than rock, sand, and most other natural substances. As a result, the surface water on the planet plays a major role in controlling both daily and seasonal weather patterns.

Before You Start

Remove any paper or plastic labels from the coffee cans so they are bare metal. Paint the outside of all coffee cans flat black and allow them to dry.

This activity is best conducted outdoors on a bright, sunny day, although it can also be conducted indoors next to a window that gets direct sunlight.

What to Do

❶ Ask students if they've ever eaten a piece of hot apple or cherry pie and accidentally burned their mouth on the pie filling, even though the crust was just warm.

❷ Explain that the reason the pie filling usually stays warmer for a longer period of time than the crust is something called *specific heat*. The specific heat of a substance is a measure of how much heat it can store. Specific heat also controls how fast an object heats up and cools down.

❸ Hold up a cup of water and a cup of sand. Ask students: Which material do you think will heat up faster? Invite students to conduct their own test. Photocopy and distribute "Some Like It Hot" (p. 52) to each student.

Some Like It Hot

Use coffee cans to test the specific heat of two common substances.

❶ Use the scale to weigh out equal amounts of sand and water. Put the sand in one black coffee can and the water in the other. Let the two cans stand in a dark area for about an hour so the sand and water reach exactly the same temperature.

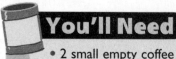

You'll Need
- 2 small empty coffee cans, painted black
- 2 lab thermometers
- Scale or balance
- Dry sand
- Water
- Watch or timer

❷ Place a lab thermometer in each can, making sure that the base of the thermometer is touching the bottom of the can. Wait one full minute and read and record the temperature of each in the chart below.

Temperature	Can with Sand	Can with Water
Starting Temperature		
After 2 Minutes		
4 Minutes		
6 Minutes		
8 Minutes		
10 Minutes		

❸ Predict: Which substance do you think will heat up first?

_____

❹ Place both cans under direct sunlight. Check the temperature every two minutes for 10 minutes. Record the temperature in the chart.

❺ After 10 minutes, take the cans out of sunlight. Which substance took longer to heat up?

_____

Think About It: Based on your experiment, why do you think the sand on the beach usually gets hotter than the water in the ocean?

Coffee Can Lung

Get It Together

- Large empty coffee can (for each group of students)
- Can opener

Science Buzz

When you inhale, your *diaphragm*, a sheet of muscle below the lungs, actually does all the breathing for you; your lungs just hold onto the air. Your chest cavity is an airtight compartment with the dome-shaped diaphragm at the bottom and the opening to your lungs at the top. When you breathe in, the diaphragm moves down, increasing the volume of the chest. This lowers the air pressure inside your body, so the outside air comes rushing in to fill the lungs. When you breathe out, the diaphragm moves up, increasing the air pressure in the chest cavity and forcing the air back out of the lungs.

Before You Start

Use a can opener to remove both ends of the coffee cans so they are hollow cylinders. Make a model Coffee Can Lung to share with students (see page 54).

What to Do

❶ Introduce the activity by having students place their hands on their abdomens and breathe in and out several times. Ask: What do you think helps you breathe? *(The respiratory system, i.e., nose or mouth, windpipe or trachea, lungs, and so on.)*

❷ Show students your model of the Coffee Can Lung. Tell students that the plastic bag inside represents the lung, and the balloon stretched at the bottom represents a dome-shaped sheet of muscle called the *diaphragm*. Explain that the diaphragm contracts and relaxes to draw air into the lungs and push it out again.

❸ Have students predict what would happen if they gently pulled down on the balloon. Invite students to create their own Coffee Can Lung. Photocopy and distribute "Create a Lung" (p. 54) to each student.

Create a Lung

Use a coffee can and a plastic bag to make a model lung.

❶ Place the plastic bag inside the can and drape the edge around the top of the cylinder. The bag should be fairly loose inside the can. Secure the bag in place with two large rubber bands.

❷ Cut off the balloon's open tip so that you're left with a large piece of curved rubber. Stretch the balloon over the bottom of the can and secure it with two rubber bands.

❸ Predict: What do you think would happen if you pulled down on the balloon at the bottom of the can?

_____

_____

_____

❹ Grasp the balloon at the bottom of the can and gently pull down. What happens? What do you think is going on?

_____

_____

_____

❺ Gently push the balloon up into the can. What happens this time? Why do you think that is?

_____

_____

_____

Think About It: Using the Coffee Can Lung as a model, how do you think human lungs work?

You'll Need

- Large empty coffee can* with both ends removed
- Gallon-sized plastic storage bag *
- 4 large, thick rubber bands
- 12-inch round balloon
- Scissors

*This activity can also be done with a small can and a sandwich-sized bag. The results, however, may not be as dramatic.

Coffee Can Science Scholastic Teaching Resources

Shake Can

Get It Together
- Empty coffee can with lid (for each group of students)
- Black paint
- Paintbrush
- A collection of different-shaped objects (e.g., wooden building block, Legos®, golf ball, buttons, sand, and so on)

Science Buzz
Humans are visual creatures. When it comes to identifying objects in the world around us, we depend on our sight more than any other sense. But if we lose our sense of sight (either temporarily or permanently), our other senses can also provide us with a great deal of critical information. We use sounds to identify different objects all the time. The more we train our sense of hearing to isolate and identify different sounds, the better we become at it.

Before You Start
Paint all the coffee can lids black so students will not be able to see through them while conducting the activity. Make a model Shake Can to share with students (see page 56).

What to Do
❶ Ask students to close their eyes and listen carefully. Stand in the middle of the room and snap your fingers. Ask: What am I doing? (*Snapping your fingers*)

❷ Ask students: How did you know what I was doing? (*Students' sense of hearing coupled with the familiar nature of the sound made it easy to identify.*)

❸ Explain that even though we don't depend on our hearing as much as our sight, the human sense of hearing is quite good. In fact, if you learn to listen carefully, you can even "see" objects with your ears.

❹ Show students the model Shake Can. Tell students that they will have to identify the mystery object that you have in the can simply by listening to the sound it makes. Demonstrate how to tilt the can slowly back and forth rather then shaking it violently. Encourage students to guess what's in the can. Then remove the lid to reveal the object.

❺ Invite students to conduct their own "sound test." Photocopy and distribute "Seeing With Sound" (p. 56) to each student.

Seeing With Sound

Use your sense of sound to identify a mystery object in a coffee can.

❶ Have your partner select a "mystery object" and place it in the coffee can. (Your partner can put in more than one of the same object.) Have him or her reseal the can with the black lid without letting you see the object.

You'll Need

- Empty coffee can with lid painted black
- A collection of different-shaped objects (e.g., wooden building block, Legos®, golf ball, buttons, sand, and so on)
- A partner

❷ Take the can in your hands and slowly tilt it back and forth. DO NOT SHAKE THE CAN HARD! Listen to the sound that the object in the can makes. How many objects are in the can? How do you know?

_____

❸ Does the mystery object roll or slide? What does this tell you about the shape of the object?

_____

❹ Listen to the sound that the object makes when it hits the side of the can. What type of material is the mystery object made of?

_____

❺ As you tilt the can back and forth, how long does it take for the object to reach one side or the other? What does this tell you about the size of the mystery object?

_____

❻ Based on your experience and the data you've collected, what do you think the mystery object is?

_____

❼ Remove the lid from the can and look at the mystery object. How close was your guess?

_____

❽ Remove the mystery object from the coffee can. Switch roles with your partner and select a different mystery object to put in the can. Snap on the lid and have your partner try to guess the object.

Think About It: How can you use your sense of hearing to "see" for you?

Coffee Can Science Scholastic Teaching Resources

Scent Can

Get It Together

- Small coffee can with lid (for each group of students)
- Black paint
- Paintbrush
- Thumbtack or pushpin
- A collection of items with distinctive odors (e.g., onions, garlic, chocolate, popcorn, peppermint, and so on)
- Zipper-style plastic sandwich bags
- Fresh lemon or orange

Science Buzz

While your sense of smell is very useful for telling you about good-tasting foods, it can also help keep you safe. Your nose can usually detect even very slight scents in the air because of a process called *diffusion*. Vapors (gases) produced by substances travel through the air, spreading away from their source where they tend to be the most concentrated. By using the concentration of the smell, you can literally "follow your nose" to find a gas leak or something that's burning.

Before You Start

Thoroughly wash the coffee cans to get rid of any coffee smell. Paint all the lids black so students cannot see through them. Use a thumbtack or pushpin to punch about a dozen small holes in each lid.

Store your collection of mystery items in separate zipper-style plastic bags so their scents don't overpower the room. Make sure that none of the students is allergic to any of the objects that you will be using.

After you have finished the activity, remove all the objects from the cans and wash them out with warm soapy water to get rid of any lingering smells. Make a model Scent Can to share with students (see page 58).

What to Do

❶ Ask students to describe their favorite smell. It might be food, like chocolate chip cookies baking, or perhaps a place, like the ocean.

❷ Explain that most people's sense of smell can detect not only what something is, but from what direction the smell is coming.

❸ Have students close their eyes. Take a freshly cut lemon or orange and walk around the room. Ask students to raise their hands if they can identify the object you are holding in your hand.

❹ Show students the model Scent Can. Tell them that they have to identify the mystery object in the can simply by smelling what's inside.

❺ Invite them to conduct their own scent test! Photocopy and distribute "Using Some Scents" (p. 58) to each student.

Using Some Scents

Use your nose to identify the mystery objects inside the coffee cans.

You'll Need
- Empty coffee can with lid painted black and holes punched in it
- A collection of items with distinctive odors (e.g., onions, garlic, chocolate, popcorn, peppermint, and so on)
- A partner

❶ Have your partner select a "mystery object" and place it in the coffee can. Have him or her reseal the can with the black lid without letting you see the object.

❷ Hold the lid of the can about six inches away from your nose and gently wave your hand in the air over the can so the air carries the scent to you. (Do not stick the can right up against your nose and take a deep breath!) This procedure is called *wafting* and is used by scientists to smell unknown objects. Why do you think this is a better way to smell things?

_____

_____

❸ Predict: What do you think the mystery object in the can is?

_____

❹ Open the lid on the can and examine the object. Were you correct?

_____

❺ Remove the mystery object from the coffee can. Rinse out the can thoroughly with water to get rid of any smell. Switch roles with your partner and select another mystery object to put in the coffee can. Snap on the lid and have your partner try to guess the object.

Think About It: How does your sense of smell help protect you from dangerous substances?

Coffee Can Science Scholastic Teaching Resources

Touch Can

Get It Together
- Small empty coffee can (for each group of students)
- Duct or masking tape
- Tennis ball, golf ball, or a similar object with a distinctive texture

Science Buzz

The human sense of touch is extremely well developed. Not only do our fingers and toes help us manipulate objects, but our sense of touch often acts as our first line of defense against potentially harmful objects. Even before you grab a hot pan on the stove, your skin senses the heat and alerts you to back away. In a similar fashion, when you step on something sharp you can usually pull back before the object sticks in your foot.

Before You Start

Thoroughly wash out the coffee cans. Put a piece of duct or masking tape around each can's open rim to cover any sharp edges.

What to Do

❶ Ask students if they've ever had to find something in the dark. Maybe they were camping out in the woods at night, or maybe they didn't want to turn on a light and wake another person. Ask: When you can't see what you're doing, how do you find stuff? (*You feel for it.*)

❷ Explain that because we depend mostly on our eyes and ears, we often forget just how important our sense of touch is. Have students close their eyes and hold out their hands. Walk around the room and place a "mystery object" in students' hands. After everyone has had a chance to feel the object, have students open their eyes and guess what it was.

❸ Invite students to explore how good they are at "seeing with their hands." Photocopy and distribute "Getting the Feel of It" (p. 60) to each student.

Name _____   Date _____

Getting the Feel of It

Use your sense of touch to identify mystery objects hidden in a coffee can.

❶ Have your partner select a "mystery object" and place it in the coffee can. (Your partner can put in more than one of the same object.) Have him or her slip the can inside a large, clean tube sock so the bottom of the can is at the toe of the sock.

❷ Without looking, feel the object inside the coffee can. How many objects are in the can?

_____

❸ Describe the shape of the object(s) in the can.

_____

_____

❹ Describe the texture of the object(s) in the can.

_____

❺ What type of material do you think the mystery object is made of?

_____

❻ Predict: What do you think the mystery object is?

_____

❼ Remove the can from the sock and look at the mystery object. How close was your guess?

_____

❽ Remove the mystery object from the coffee can. Switch roles with your partner and select a different mystery object to place in the can. Place the can back inside the sock and have your partner try to guess the object.

Think About It: How can your sense of touch help you "see your way around" in a dark room?

Coffee Can Gizzard

OBJECTIVE: To demonstrate how some birds digest their food

Get It Together

- Small coffee can with lid (for each group of students)
- 2 fresh chicken gizzards (from a butcher shop)
- Sharp knife
- 2 plastic zipper-style sandwich bag
- Photo of a chicken
- Small cup of wild birdseed

Science Buzz

If you've ever looked closely at the mouths of many birds like chickens, you'll see that they have beaks, but no teeth. So how do they chew the seeds that they eat? They don't! Instead, they swallow their food whole, and then a special organ in the back of their stomach called the *gizzard* does the "chewing" for them. Gizzards actually grind food using special stones called *gastroliths* (stomach stones). The gizzard has a thick muscular wall that moves the stones back and forth, crushing the seeds and other foods.

Birds aren't the only animals that use gastroliths to help them digest food. Earthworms and bryozoans also have gizzard-like structures. And some paleontologists believe that many plant-eating dinosaurs had gizzard-like structures. They have found stones in neat piles near dinosaur skeletons. These gastroliths exhibit marks and grooves similar to the little stones found in birds' gizzards, except they're much bigger.

Before You Start

Get two fresh chicken gizzards from a local butcher shop and rinse them well. Using a knife, cut one gizzard open to expose the little gastroliths inside. Place both gizzards in a clear plastic sandwich bag and seal them. Rinse out the coffee cans to remove any residue. The cans should be clean before starting the experiment.

What to Do

❶ Hold up or pass around the picture of the chicken. Ask students: How do you think chickens chew their food when they don't have teeth? *(They just swallow food.)*

❷ Explain that when chickens eat seeds, they usually swallow their food whole and digestion happens inside their body. Pass around the cup of birdseed and invite students to take a few seeds and try to break them in their fingers. Ask students to predict what might happen to the seeds once they get in the bird's stomach. *(The seeds won't get digested easily because they are so hard.)*

❸ Explain that if chickens had to depend on their stomach muscles alone to digest their food, little, if any, digestion would happen. Fortunately they have an organ called a *gizzard*, which aids in digestion. Pass around the whole gizzard and ask students to feel it through the bag. Then pass around the gizzard that has been cut open and ask them to describe what they see inside the gizzard. They should see some tiny stones. Ask students to think about what those stones might be for.

❹ Invite students to find out how a chicken gizzard works. Photocopy and distribute "Gizzards and Stones" (p. 62) to each student.

Gizzards and Stones

Use a coffee can and some stones to see how a chicken digests its food.

❶ Examine the dry rice closely. Pour it along with the water into the coffee can. Seal the lid tight and shake the can vigorously for two minutes.

You'll Need

- Small clean coffee can with lid
- Large clear plastic cup with 6 oz. of water
- $1/4$ cup dry rice
- Small plastic bowl
- 5 or 6 small pebbles ($1/2$- to 1-inch in diameter)
- Watch or timer

❷ Carefully pour the contents of the can into the plastic bowl and examine them closely. Describe how the rice looks. Do you see any change to the rice grains since you first put them into the can?

_____

_____

❸ Pour the rice and water mixture back into the coffee can. This time add five or six small pebbles to the can. Seal the can tightly with the lid and shake the can vigorously for another two minutes. Predict: What will happen to the rice this time?

_____

_____

❹ Empty the contents of the can back into the bowl and examine the rice again. How has the rice changed?

_____

_____

Think About It: How do gastroliths or "stomach stones" help chickens digest their food?